Study Guide

QUIT CHURCH

Because Your Life Would Be Better If You Did

Cover design: Sara Young
Cover photo: Brenton Stanley

ISBN: 978-1-960678-46-1   1 2 3 4 5 6 7 8 9 10

Printed in the United States of America

Study Guide

QUIT CHURCH

Because Your Life Would Be Better If You Did

CHRIS SONKSEN

ARROWS &
STONES

CONTENTS

QUIT HOPING TO WAKE UP IN HEAVEN

Quit looking for the perfect church; it isn't out there.

READING TIME

As you read Chapter 1: "Quit Hoping to Wake Up in Heaven" in *Quit Church*, review, reflect on, and respond to the text by answering the following questions.

REFLECT AND TAKE ACTION:

Have you ever been frustrated by something church-related that didn't go the way you had hoped? What was it? In your own words, why is this dangerous?

_____

_____

_____

_____

_____

_____

_____

_____

Do you think it's important for people to have loyalty? Why or why not?

_____

_____

_____

_____

_____

_____

_____

_____

> *What is causing the quarrels and fights among you? Don't they come from the evil desires at war within you?*
>
> —James 4:1

Consider the scripture above and answer the following questions:

What is the meaning of this verse, in your own words?

_____

_____

_____

_____

_____

_____

_____

_____

What does this verse reveal to us about our quarrels with our brothers and sisters?

_____

_____

_____

_____

_____

_____

_____

_____

Of the three different areas of tension (church matters, spiritual matters, personal matters), which do you think is the most common? Why are these three categories separated?

_____

_____

_____

_____

_____

_____

_____

_____

_____

_____

What occurs when church members and attendees are loyal? How does the church benefit?

_____

_____

_____

_____

_____

_____

_____

_____

_____

_____

Think about a time you were left confused, unsettled, or with feelings of division following a conversation you had in or relating to church. How did you respond to this situation? How could you have responded better?

_____

_____

_____

_____

_____

_____

_____

_____

_____

_____

Considering that the church is the bride of Christ, what steps can you take to better protect, guard, and honor the church?

_____

_____

_____

_____

_____

_____

_____

_____

_____

_____

What have you done recently that has shown support for your pastor and church leaders?

_____

_____

_____

_____

_____

_____

_____

_____

_____

_____

QUIT CHURCH

CHAPTER 2

QUIT GIVING YOUR MONEY AWAY

*If you are not careful, you
will put more trust in your
savings than in your Savior.*

READING TIME

As you read Chapter 2: "Quit Giving Your Money Away" in *Quit Church*, review, reflect on, and respond to the text by answering the following questions.

REFLECT AND TAKE ACTION:

Have you ever been hesitant to tithe because you didn't know where the money was going? Explain the situation.

_____

_____

_____

_____

_____

_____

_____

_____

In your own words, why do we tithe? What is the purpose of tithing and why is it our responsibility?

_____

_____

_____

_____

_____

_____

_____

_____

Have you ever viewed the money you've been blessed with as your "protector" or "provider"? Why or why not? If you answered yes, do you still view it like this?

_____

_____

_____

_____

_____

_____

_____

_____

> *The heavens are yours, and the earth is yours; everything in the world is yours—you created it all.*
>
> —Psalm 89:11

Consider the scripture above and answer the following questions:

What do you feel is the meaning of this verse?

_____

_____

_____

_____

_____

_____

_____

How does this verse relate to tithing? Is the money God's, the church's, or the individual's?

_____

_____

_____

_____

_____

_____

_____

_____

_____

In what ways does God help us "win" when we are faithful and give?

_____

_____

_____

_____

_____

_____

_____

_____

_____

_____

What is the "success cycle" discussed in this chapter? Are you getting caught up on one of these cycle stages?

_____
_____
_____
_____
_____
_____
_____
_____
_____
_____

Consider the statement "He is either Lord of all or not at all." Is God Lord over all areas of your life? In what areas is He not in control? Explain your answer.

_____
_____
_____
_____
_____
_____
_____
_____
_____
_____

What matters do you need to settle in your heart today regarding your finances or personal walk with God?

_____

_____

_____

_____

_____

_____

_____

_____

_____

_____

Where can you make a positive change in this area? Take some time to pray by yourself or in a group. Make a verbal commitment about the change you will make moving forward.

_____

_____

_____

_____

_____

_____

_____

_____

_____

_____

QUIT HELPING OUT

*Your church has places for you to serve,
and Christ wants you to serve there.*

READING TIME

As you read Chapter 3: "Quit Helping Out" in
Quit Church, review, reflect on, and respond to
the text by answering the following questions.

REFLECT AND TAKE ACTION:

Why do you think it is important to serve the church?
What does service mean and why do we do it?

_____

_____

_____

_____

_____

_____

_____

Have you ever felt your service was unneeded
or unappreciated? Did this discourage you from
serving in the future? Explain your answer.

_____

_____

_____

_____

_____

_____

_____

_____

> *So stop telling lies. Let us tell our neighbors the truth, for we are all parts of the same body.*
>
> —Ephesians 4:25

Consider the scripture above and answer the following questions:

What does this verse reveal about how the church operates?

_____

_____

_____

_____

_____

_____

_____

How do serving others and recognizing that we are different parts of the same body tie together? Explain.

_____

_____

_____

_____

_____

_____

_____

_____

Are there times when you stand on the sidelines and wait for others to serve? Why do you think you do this?

_____

_____

_____

_____

_____

_____

_____

_____

_____

_____

Is there a service opportunity you know God is nudging you toward? What is it? Explain.

_____

_____

_____

_____

_____

_____

_____

_____

_____

_____

_____

What was your best serving experience? How did it impact others? How did it make you feel? How did it affect you?

_____

_____

_____

_____

_____

_____

_____

_____

_____

_____

Where could you start serving this week? In what area(s) do you see a need? Find a place to start serving and commit to beginning this week.

_____

_____

_____

_____

_____

_____

_____

_____

_____

_____

_____

Notes:

_____

_____

_____

_____

_____

_____

_____

_____

_____

_____

_____

_____

_____

_____

_____

_____

_____

_____

_____

_____

_____

_____

_____

_____

_____

_____

_____

_____

QUIT HOPING PEOPLE WILL COME

*Love them enough to share what
you know will change their life.*

READING TIME

As you read Chapter 4: "Quit Hoping People Will Come" in *Quit Church*, review, reflect on, and respond to the text by answering the following questions.

REFLECT AND TAKE ACTION:

How do you go about inviting new individuals to your church? Do you feel this is effective?

_____

_____

_____

_____

_____

_____

_____

When it comes to getting new people to attend your church, are you following God's strategy or your own? How can you be so sure?

_____

_____

_____

_____

_____

_____

_____

_____

What, if anything, is holding your church back from more attendees? Fear of inviting others? Lack of confidence? Uncertainty?

_____

_____

_____

_____

_____

_____

_____

_____

_____

> *When Jesus heard this, he said, "Healthy people don't need a doctor—sick people do."*
>
> *—Matthew 9:12*

Consider the scripture above and answer the following questions:

What do you think Jesus meant when He said this?

_____

_____

_____

_____

_____

_____

_____

_____

What does this verse reveal about who we should be ministering to and inviting to church?

_____

_____

_____

_____

_____

_____

_____

_____

_____

_____

Who do you think Christ means by "healthy people"?

_____

_____

_____

_____

_____

_____

_____

_____

_____

_____

_____

What has your concept of evangelism been? How have you seen it done or experienced it?

_____

_____

_____

_____

_____

_____

_____

_____

_____

Have you been like Matthew in your realm of influence? If yes, explain how. If no, explain how you could draw closer to Matthew's example.

_____

_____

_____

_____

_____

_____

_____

_____

_____

In your own words, define the "invest" and "invite" concepts discussed in this chapter. How can you implement these into your strategy?

_____

_____

_____

_____

_____

_____

_____

_____

What does it really mean to "include" someone once you've invested and invited them?

_____

_____

_____

_____

_____

_____

_____

Who can you start with in your circle of influence? Make a list of people you can begin to invest in and ultimately invite to church. Be intentional to reach out to them this week.

_____

_____

_____

_____

_____

_____

_____

QUIT STOPPING BY

God takes note of those who are dependable, and He rewards those who are faithful.

READING TIME

As you read Chapter 5: "Quit Stopping By" in *Quit Church*, review, reflect on, and respond to the text by answering the following questions.

REFLECT AND TAKE ACTION:

What is dependability? Do you look for this trait in the people you hire, look up to, and surround yourself with?

_____

_____

_____

_____

_____

_____

_____

_____

Why do you think dependability is such an important characteristic in the church? What value does it bring?

_____

_____

_____

_____

_____

_____

_____

What is "predetermined dependability"? Do you possess this?

_____

_____

_____

_____

_____

_____

_____

_____

_____

> *As long as Moses held up the staff in his hand, the Israelites had the advantage. But whenever he dropped his hand, the Amalekites gained the advantage.*
>
> —Exodus 17:11

Consider the scripture above and answer the following questions:

What stands out to you from this verse?

_____

_____

_____

_____

_____

_____

_____

Do you think Moses' situation is similar to your
situation today? Explain your answer.

_____

_____

_____

_____

_____

_____

_____

_____

_____

_____

Was Moses giving the advantage to the Israelites,
or was God? Couldn't God have done this without
Moses' involvement? Explain.

_____

_____

_____

_____

_____

_____

_____

_____

_____

_____

What are some of the ways that churches benefit from consistency and dependability?

_____

_____

_____

_____

_____

_____

_____

_____

_____

_____

_____

Where in your life have you shown dependability to others? In what areas can you do a better job of being dependable?

_____

_____

_____

_____

_____

_____

_____

_____

_____

_____

_____

On a scale of 1-10, how would you rate your dependability to your church family each week? Would they give you the same rating? Explain your answer.

1   2   3   4   5   6   7   8   9   10

_____

_____

_____

_____

_____

_____

_____

_____

_____

_____

In what ways can you emulate Aaron and Hur in your extended family at church?

_____

_____

_____

_____

_____

_____

_____

_____

_____

QUIT YOUR CHURCH FRIENDS

We need connection, relationship, and community with each other. It's the way God designed us.

READING TIME

As you read Chapter 6: "Quit Your Church Friends" in *Quit Church*, review, reflect on, and respond to the text by answering the following questions.

REFLECT AND TAKE ACTION:

Have you ever been blind to your intrinsic need for community? If so, what was the result?

_____

_____

_____

_____

_____

_____

_____

Do you ever feel "too busy" to work on the relationships in your life? Explain a time you've felt this or something similar.

_____

_____

_____

_____

_____

_____

_____

_____

What is fellowship and why is it important? Where do you go besides church on Sunday mornings for fellowship?

_____

_____

_____

_____

_____

_____

And all the believers met together in one place and shared everything they had. They sold their property and possessions and shared the money with those in need. They worshipped together at the Temple each day, met in homes for the Lord's Supper, and shared their meals with great joy and generosity. . . .

—Acts 2:44-46

Consider the scripture above and answer the following questions:

Does your church mirror how united the early church was according to this verse?

_____

_____

_____

_____

_____

_____

_____

What about the early church stands out to you from
this passage?

_____

_____

_____

_____

_____

_____

_____

_____

_____

_____

What do you struggle with the most when building
relationships and/or friendships?

_____

_____

_____

_____

_____

_____

_____

_____

_____

_____

_____

How many relationships do you have with others in
your church? 10? 50? 200?

_____

_____

_____

_____

_____

_____

_____

_____

_____

_____

_____

How can you be more effective relationally in your
church today? Be realistic.

_____

_____

_____

_____

_____

_____

_____

_____

_____

_____

_____

Can you see the difference in your life when you're in healthy relationships in the church versus when you're not? Explain your answer. What is different?

_____

_____

_____

_____

_____

_____

_____

_____

_____

_____

What step can you commit to today to have healthier and stronger relationships with people in your church family? Make the step practical and attainable.

_____

_____

_____

_____

_____

_____

_____

_____

_____

_____

_____

www.ingramcontent.com/pod-product-compliance
Lightning Source LLC
Chambersburg PA
CBHW070051100426
42734CB00040B/2984